A Weird History of Science

Foolish Physics

John Townsend

www.raintreepublishers.co.uk
Visit our website to find out more information about **Raintree** books.

To order:
☎ Phone 44 (0) 1865 888112
📄 Send a fax to 44 (0) 1865 314091
💻 Visit the Raintree bookshop at **www.raintreepublishers.co.uk** to browse our catalogue and order online.

MONKEY PUZZLE MEDIA LTD

Produced for Raintree by
Monkey Puzzle Media Ltd
Gissing's Farm, Fressingfield
Suffolk IP21 5SH, UK

First published in Great Britain by Raintree,
Halley Court, Jordan Hill, Oxford OX2 8EJ,
part of Harcourt Education.
Raintree is a registered trademark
of Harcourt Education Ltd.

Editor: Steve Parker
Designer: Tim Mayer
Illustrator: Michael Posen
Picture Researcher: Lynda Lines
Production: Chloe Bloom
Originated by Modern Age
Printed and bound in China
by South China Printing Company

10 digit ISBN 1 4062 0557 5
13 digit ISBN 978 1 4062 0557 2
11 10 09 08 07
10 9 8 7 6 5 4 3 2 1

**British Library Cataloguing in
Publication Data**
Townsend, John, 1955–
Foolish physics. – (A weird history of science)
Physics – History – Juvenile literature
I.Title
530.9

Acknowledgements
AKG-Images p. **40**; Alamy Images p. **39**
(Stockfolio); Corbis pp. **1** (Sergei Remezov/
Reuters), **5 bottom right** (Museum of the City
of New York), **19** (Bettmann), **30** (Museum of
the City of New York), **42** (Bettmann), **48** (Sergei
Remezov/Reuters); Getty Images pp. **23**
(PhotoDisc), **24**, **41** (AFP), **44** (Hulton Archive),
46 (PhotoDisc); Illustrated London News Picture
Library p. **32**; Mary Evans Picture Library pp. **7**,
31; MPM Images p. **17** (Digital Vision), **37**
(Creativ Collection); NASA pp. **5 left** (Reto
Stockli, Alan Nelson, Fritz Hasler), **13** (ESA/Erich
Karkoschka, University of Arizona), **15**, **18**
(Marshall Space Flight Center), **22** (Marshall
Space Flight Center); Science and Society Picture
Library pp. **21** (Science Museum, London);
Science Photo Library pp. **5 top right**, **5
middle right** (Mikki Rain), **6** (Sheila Terry), **8**,
12 (Sheila Terry), **16** (Mikki Rain), **25** (NASA),
26 (Sheila Terry), **27**, **28**, **29** (Sheila Terry), **33**
(Peter Menzel), **34**, **35** (Peter Menzel), **36**, **38**
(Tom McHugh), **45** (Martin Bond), **47** (Philippe
Plailly), **49** (Victor Habbick Visions); Jules Selmes
p. **43**; Topfoto.co.uk pp. **4**, **9**, **10** (ANA/Image
Works), **11**, **20**.

Cover photograph of a hair-raising experiment
with a small electrical generator reproduced with
permission of Getty Images/Time & Life Pictures.

Every effort has been made to contact copyright
holders of any material reproduced in this book.
Any omissions will be rectified in subsequent
printings if notice is given to the publishers.

Contents

Any words appearing in the text in bold,
like this, are explained in the glossary.
You can also look out for them in the Word
bank at the bottom of each page.

Risky science

Science has always been full of risks. To answer questions like "How does the world work?", scientists often ended up in big trouble. As they dabbled with danger in scary experiments, some scientists got hurt – or worse. Some made silly mistakes and others poked fun at them. A few came up with ideas that went against the beliefs of the time, which upset people and put the scientists at risk of attack.

Despite such hazards, science has led to some amazing ideas and weird discoveries. Daring experiments have cost some scientists their lives, as they tried to unravel secrets of the Universe. Many of those secrets still remain.

Young Albert Einstein, who would become one of the most famous physicists of all time, said: "Science is a wonderful thing if one does not have to earn one's living at it."

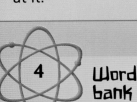

Word bank

atom smallest piece or particle of a substance
force push or pull that makes things move or change direction

Fantastic physics

Our lives would be very different today without physicists. These scientists study bits of **matter** like **atoms**. They also try to understand heat, light, electricity, motion, and **forces** such as gravity. Their work has helped to make today's world possible with electricity, television, computers, cars, planes, rockets, and satellites.

Despite such discoveries, people often think that physicists must be slightly strange. They work in their **laboratories** with mind-boggling machines, frightening forces and fearsome **formulas**. But is the world of foolish physics really so freaky and peculiar? You may be surprised to find out just how weird the history of science could be...

For hundreds of years, the science of physics has tried to unravel the secrets of Earth and the Universe.

Find out later

Which major physics discovery happened in a bathroom?

What did a great scientist discover under an apple tree?

Which scientist nearly killed himself in a thunderstorm?

formula process or rule written as numbers, letters, and symbols
matter substance made of atoms and similar particles

In the beginning

Ancient accidents

Stone Age people from many thousands of years ago were early scientists. They tested materials such as wood, stones, bones, and skins, to find the best ones for weapons, tools, and clothes. They made mistakes but they also learned what worked, as they found out the various **properties** of different materials.

The science of physics has always tried to understand the Earth – where it came from, its size and shape, and how it works inside. About 3,500 years ago people in what is now the Middle East thought the world was a flat disc floating on a giant sea. Around 2,500 years ago Greek maps pictured the Earth flat like a pancake.

About 2,350 years ago Greek scientist and thinker Aristotle explained how the Earth was a huge ball. His idea caught on. There are stories about sailors from just a few hundred years ago who feared that they would sail off the edge of a flat Earth. These stories were probably not true. Nearly all people believed in a round Earth long before then.

This world map from almost 500 years ago, by famous mapmaker Albrecht Dürer, was the best of its time. It showed that people knew Earth was round.

Word bank

indivisible impossible to split into smaller parts

Ancient antics in the air

It took thousands of years for people to discover some of the basic laws of nature. The earliest people watched birds and wondered how they flew. Some scientists attached feathers or wooden wings to their arms and tried to fly.

The results were disastrous. The "birdmen" found out the hard way that human arms are not strong enough to flap like real wings. Until scientists understood about gravity and motion, people had no chance of getting airborne. Only very recently in history have people used physics to make flying machines.

Big ideas on small particles

Democritus was a Greek scientist who lived over 2,350 years ago. He said that cutting a stone into smaller and smaller pieces would, in the end, make bits so tiny that they could no longer be divided. He called such tiny bits *atomos*, meaning **"indivisible"**. It took another 2,000 years for most scientists to agree with him.

Democritus (460–357 BC) suggested that all substances and matter were made of tiny pieces, which he named **"atoms"**.

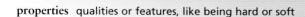

Leaping from the bath

Archimedes was a great scientist and mathematician in Greece more than 2,200 years ago. Some people thought he was strange – not just because he had so many new ideas, but because he could get very excited when he found an answer to a question.

The king asked Archimedes to solve a problem. Was his crown solid gold, or a cheap metal covered with a thin gold layer? Archimedes couldn't work out how to tell without scratching the crown and damaging it. Then one evening he sat in his bath and the water sloshed over the sides – the answer came to him in a flash.

Archimedes suddenly worked out his physics problem while getting into his bath and watching the water rise.

Word bank

density   amount of material or matter in a certain volume

Got it!

Archimedes weighed the crown. He got a piece of gold of the same weight. He put each in turn into a bowl full of water and compared how much water spilled out. He saw that the gold piece pushed aside or displaced less water than the crown. This was because of **density**. The gold was more dense than the metal of the crown – that is, the same weight of it took up less volume or space.

In this way Archimedes proved that the crown was a fake. It was not gold, but a cheap gold-looking metal. It was worth leaping out of the bath for some simple physics!

Archimedes' ideas about density have helped scientists to check the gold in precious treasures. This is the gold mask of Tutankhamun from ancient Egypt.

9

Stars of the Middle Ages

For hundreds of years after the ancient Greeks, scientists who studied the stars believed that the Earth was the centre of the Universe. The Christian Church also taught that the Sun, Moon, and stars all moved around the Earth.

We now know the Earth moves around the Sun. Polish scientist Nicolaus Copernicus (1473–1543) worked out that the Sun is at the centre of the **Solar System**. By studying movements of the Sun, Moon, and stars across the sky, he proved that the centre of the Solar System was "in the Sun, or near it". However his ideas outraged the Church.

Middle Ages

The years from about AD 600 to AD 1500 are now called the Middle Ages or the Medieval Period. During this time people who tried to understand the Earth, Sun, Moon, and stars often got into trouble. The Christian Church in Europe was very powerful and it did not like scientists challenging the Bible.

Nicolaus Copernicus used models to help him work out the position of Earth, the other planets, and the Sun.

Word bank   astronomer scientist who studies stars, moons, planets, and other space objects

Tycho Brahe (right) worked with his assistant Johannes Kepler (left) on many puzzles in astronomy. Kepler became even more famous than Brahe (see page 12).

Did you know?

In 2005 historians found bones in a grave in Poland where they thought Copernicus was buried. Using the skull, experts built up a face to show how the man once looked. They said: "We can be almost 100 per cent sure this is Copernicus." He had a broken nose and a scar over his right eye.

Bursting with ideas – and more

Danish scientist Tycho Brahe (1546–1601) developed the ideas of Copernicus. Tycho recorded in detail what he saw every night in the sky. He made special equipment for studying the stars and planets, and his measurements were very accurate.

Apart from being the greatest **astronomer** of his time, Tycho was also known for losing his nose in a sword fight. He wore a false metal nose instead! His death was famous, too. Apparently he was at a feast where he drank too much. He was too polite to ask to be excused. He had trouble passing urine from his full bladder, and died slowly over the next eleven days.

Tycho's beliefs

Tycho Brahe had a very clever German assistant called Johannes Kepler (1571–1630). He was one of the first people to study what we now call **astrophysics**. But, like most others of his time, he also believed in **astrology** – the magical powers of the stars over people's lives. He drew hundreds of star charts for telling the future. He wrote about his ideas to the greatest scientist of his day, Galileo Galilei (1564–1642).

From 1609 Galileo used his telescope to make many discoveries, including seeing mountains on the Moon for the first time.

Galileo in trouble

Galileo built one of the earliest telescopes – but what he saw through it got him into great trouble. He noticed three bright "stars" moving around Jupiter. If these stars weren't moving around the Earth, then the Earth couldn't be the centre of everything. Perhaps Copernicus was right about the Sun being the centre.

Galileo wrote about this discovery, but he knew it would upset the Church. Even so, he took the risk of publishing his ideas. In those days it was a crime to question the teaching of the Bible so he was arrested – all because of physics. He was locked up in prison at first. Later he was kept under house arrest in Florence, Italy, until he died nine years later.

Punishment

Galileo was threatened with torture by Church leaders. To avoid this he had to confess that his idea about the Earth moving around the Sun was wrong. Finally he agreed that the Earth didn't move – but then apparently he whispered: "And yet, it does move." In 1983, the Church finally agreed that Galileo might have been right after all.

These three dark spots on planet Jupiter are shadows cast on to its surface by its tiny moons – the same moons that set Galileo thinking.

astrophysics branch of science dealing with physical and chemical measurements of stars and other huge objects in space

Beating gravity

Falling to Earth

One of the many hopeful fliers of history was a monk called Eilmer. About 1,000 years ago he "flew" for 200 metres (656 feet). But it was more of a glide since he jumped from a tower in Malmesbury, England with wings strapped to his body. He swooped down, crashed, and broke both legs.

Humans have always dreamed of floating or flying far above the ground. But, no matter how many times people covered themselves in feathers and jumped out of trees, they just couldn't stay in the sky. Scientists began to ask questions about flight. Why can't humans fly? What **force** keeps everything in its place on the ground? Why do objects fall downwards?

There are tales of the great Galileo spending hours dropping cannonballs and other things from the Leaning Tower of Pisa in Italy, to find out what happened. He saw that objects of different weights fell at the same speed, which was a surprise for the time. It was interesting science but it didn't help anyone to fly.

Eilmer the monk could only glide on his home-made wings. His "flight" in the year AD 1010 may have looked something like this.

Word bank

propulsion   pushing power, a force that makes something move

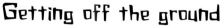

Getting off the ground

No one knows how many people through history have tied wings to their arms – and crashed to the ground. Chinese stories tell of people trying to sail through the air attached to kites. Yet before machines could fly, scientists had to understand three important laws (see right). It took many centuries to make a machine that was light, strong, powerful, and streamlined enough to beat the force of gravity.

Just so you know

The force that keeps our feet firmly on the ground is gravity. This is one of the most basic forces of nature. Earth's gravity pulls everything towards the centre of the planet. Without the force of gravity, nothing would stay in place on the ground – objects would float around and zoom off in space.

Flying high

Three kinds of science are important in making a flying machine.

- Aerodynamics – how air flows around a flying object.
- **Propulsion** – how a force can make something move and keep it moving.
- Structure – how a craft is built from materials that are strong but light enough to stay in the air.

Out in space, the force of Earth's gravity is almost zero. So people and things float about as though weightless.

15

Falling apples

Isaac Newton (1642–1727) was one of the greatest of all scientists. He was clever at maths and worked out all kinds of **theories** about light, **astronomy**, and gravity.

It seems that Newton was a born scientist, because even as a child he was always trying to find out what made things happen. When a storm was blowing one night, Newton's mother sent him to check their farm and make sure all the gates were secure. When he didn't come back, his mother went looking for him. She found him jumping off a fence to see how far the wind would carry him!

Apples on the mind

A story about Isaac Newton told how he was sitting in his garden in 1664, aged 22 years, when an apple fell from a tree on to his head. He asked a simple question: Why did the apple come down and not go up? He began to study this force that made things fall – leading to some of the greatest ideas in physics.

Was the story about an apple falling on Newton's head true? He only told it to friends in about 1726, near the end of his life.

Word bank

calculation detailed mathematical work
genius very gifted person with great abilities

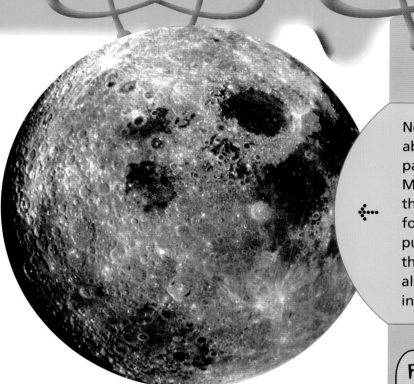

Newton's ideas about gravity came partly from the Moon. He imagined the mysterious force not only pulling objects to the ground, but also extending far into space.

Funny physics

Isaac Newton made many great advances in the study of gravity, motion, light, and other areas of science. However other people didn't know what to make of him. Was he a **genius** or just freaky? Later in life Newton did seem to become very strange. He had bitter arguments with other scientists and refused to talk to some of them.

Heavy thinking

When Newton thought about why things fell to the ground, he was beginning his work on the **force** of gravity. He asked questions like: What makes things fall? Can anything stop objects from falling? Are the Sun, Moon, and stars falling? If so, why don't they ever hit the ground?

Newton spent years answering these questions by thinking, making **calculations** and doing experiments. He developed his law of gravity to explain how the Earth pulls objects towards itself, depending on how heavy and how far away they are. He explained how planets move around the Sun and how moons move around planets. It was ground-breaking physics.

theory general idea to explain how something happens

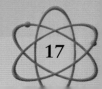

Rocket science

About 500 years ago a Chinese scientist called Wan Hu tried to get off the ground using the great **force** provided by rockets. The story tells how Wan Hu wanted to be the first **astronaut**. He made a rocket-powered flying chair with two large kites tied to it. He strapped himself to the chair and told his servants, each with a flaming torch, to light the 47 rocket fuses. There was a huge BANG. When the smoke finally cleared, there was nothing left. Wan Hu and his chair were blown to bits.

First flying machines

More than 1,500 years ago, people in China made simple "helicopter" toys that twirled through the air. The Italian artist and designer Leonardo da Vinci (1452–1519) showed a good understanding of science by designing several kinds of flying machines. It is unlikely these were actually made, although some could have worked like a modern-day hang-glider.

Wan Hu's journey to the stars didn't quite go to plan – his chair exploded.

Word bank

astronaut traveller in space

Up and away

In 1781 Karl Fredrich Meerwein, a German designer, built, and flew his own flapping-winged machine. However, people who saw him reported that the craft was really a glider. It could not stay in the air using the power of its flapping wings.

Two years later another craft took off, this time using hot air – which rises with smoke from a fire. The Montgolfier brothers of France made a balloon filled with hot air from a blazing fire underneath. The balloon carried a sheep, a duck, and a cockerel in a basket, to show it was possible to survive in the sky. The brothers clearly didn't want to risk going up themselves!

Scary science

In 1782 the Montgolfier brothers discovered that heated air collected inside a lightweight fabric bag caused the bag to rise. After the animal flight, humans first took off in 1783. Two men in a Montgolfier balloon flew from Paris, France. They stayed up for 25 minutes and landed safely about 9 kilometres (5.6 miles) away.

The first people to fly in a hot-air balloon were Pîlatre de Rozier and the Marquis d'Arlandes. Did the Montgolfier brothers not trust their own craft?

Fighting gravity

The battle against gravity continued through the 1800s, as scientists tried to design a machine to keep a human in the air. In 1853 George Cayley made a flying machine that could carry a person. It flew for about 275 metres (600 feet) across a valley. This was the first recorded air journey, but the craft was only gliding and did not have its own power.

From about 1890 in Germany, engineer Otto Lilienthal began flights in gliders he designed himself. He even built a hill for take-off. Sadly he died in a terrible crash.

How wrong could they be?

"Man will not fly for 50 years" said Wilbur Wright in 1901. Two years later he proved himself wrong. With his brother Orville, he built and flew the first ever aeroplane, *Flyer I* (sometimes called *Kitty Hawk*). Orville made the first flight in North Carolina, United States. Five years later he said: "No flying machine will ever fly from New York to Paris." Again, within 20 years he was proved wrong.

After more than 2,500 flights in craft that resemble hang-gliders, Otto Lilienthal was killed in 1896. He lost control in a sudden strong wind and crashed into the ground.

20

Danger in the air

Some of these early attempts to master the science of flight ended in disaster. Louis Charles Letur of France built a parachute-glider. He flew it in 1853, soon after Cayley's flight. The following year, Letur crashed in London and died of his injuries.

In 1874 Belgian shoemaker and scientist Vincent De Groof designed a machine with beating wings and a parachute. His plan was to cut it loose from a balloon and glide down slowly. But the wings collapsed and he fell like a stone to his death.

In 1895 British scientist William Thomson, Lord Kelvin, said: "Heavier-than-air flying machines are impossible." Eight years later he was proved wrong – by brothers called Wright (see opposite)!

Fast-flap failure

In 1902, British inventor Edward Purkis Frost made a flying machine with large crow-like wings. They were made of willow, silk, and feathers and were very light. Sadly, Frost wasn't. Even though the wings beat 100 times a minute, the machine never took off.

In 1904 Frost was still experimenting with his ornithopter (flapping-wing flying machine). Yet the Wright brothers had made their historic flight the year before.

To the Moon

In 1668 Isaac Newton built a new type of telescope with a curved mirror. **Astronomers** could see the Moon much more clearly, and wondered what it was like there. However they thought such a trip was impossible. To design a spacecraft, they had to work out its size and speed, and how much fuel it needed. There was also the problem of how to get back to Earth.

For new physics like this, new kinds of **calculations** were needed, based on how objects move in space. Newton himself began this type of science with his laws of motion. He even invented a new type of maths, called calculus, to get it going. After several false starts, rocket science took off in the 1920s with American engineer Robert Goddard (1882–1945).

Robert Goddard launched his early rockets from his aunt's farm in Auburn, Massachusetts, United States. The first flight, of a rocket named "Nell", lasted less than three seconds.

Word bank

NASA National Aeronautics and Space Administration, responsible for the space programme of the United States since 1958

Earth-shattering science

Goddard launched the world's first liquid-fuelled rocket in 1926. Unlike a fireworks rocket, its flight could be controlled. Goddard is now considered to be the founder of modern rocketry.

German scientist Wernher von Braun (1912–1977) continued rocket development. He worked in the United States for **NASA** on the Apollo space flights. In 1969 the age-old dream came true with Apollo 11 when two men, Neil Armstrong and Buzz Aldrin, walked on the Moon.

First moon landing

Astronauts first walked on the Moon in July 1969. Millions of people watched live television pictures all around the world. This was seen as one of the greatest scientific achievements of all time. As Neil Armstrong stepped on to the Moon's surface he said: "That's one small step for a man, one giant leap for mankind."

Twelve astronauts have walked on the Moon, bringing back over 380 kilograms (836 pounds) of rocks and dust for scientists to study.

23

Back with a bump

Ever since rocket science began, people dreamed of reaching Mars. The "Red Planet" has always amazed us and many scientists hope that humans will walk on Mars one day. Getting that far depends on a lot of physics – and money. It takes more than six months to get to Mars, and the same time to return. Missions to Mars without people aboard have succeeded and taught scientists a great deal about our nearest planet.

Costly physics blunder

When the Mars Climate Orbiter spacecraft was launched in 1998, scientists hoped to find just what it was like on the planet. However they made a blunder. They measured distances in feet and miles, while the computer that steered the **probe** in space worked in metres and kilometres. The probe went missing in 1999. Oops!

Just so you know

The distance between the Earth and Mars varies according to where they are in their long journeys around the Sun. At their closest they are about 56 million kilometres (35 million miles) apart. Their greatest distance is about seven times further, at 400 million kilometres (250 million miles). So it helps to plan a Mars trip many years ahead.

The Climate Orbiter craft was supposed to measure the weather on Mars and photograph the planet's polar regions. However the radio link with it was lost.

probe small unmanned spacecraft

Human error

In 2001 **NASA** launched a spacecraft called Genesis. Its three-year mission was to travel into deep space, during which it collected about 20 micrograms (just less than one-millionth of an ounce) of "space dust" – the weight of a few salt grains. The spaceship did this task successfully. Then it closed its collecting lids and headed back to Earth so that physicists could study the material.

In September 2004 the last few seconds of the long Genesis project went very wrong. The craft's parachutes failed to open. It crashed into the Utah Desert in the United States and broke open on impact, and some of the space dust was lost.

Two rovers as big as quad bikes have trundled about on Mars since 2004, taking photographs. This photo shows Martian dust, rocks (on the right) and the tent-sized landing craft cover (left). A rare success – a Mars mission that worked!

Crackling electrics

Did you know?

On dry days, static electricity can build up in our bodies and clothes. It causes sparks to jump from us to pieces of metal like a car or door handle, or to other people's bodies. On damp days the moisture in the air carries away the electricity so it does not build up.

In many homes today you just flick a switch and get instant light, heat, and power. By plugging into a socket we can use the flowing **energy** that scientists have studied for centuries – electricity. Just 150 years ago, this was unheard of.

Ever since scientists saw lightning or touched electric fish, they have tried to make, store, and control electrical energy. Because of such work, we now accept electricity without much thought. In the past, many people thought bolts of lightning were warnings from the gods. They couldn't explain why rubbed pieces of cloth attracted feathers or what happened when someone's clothes sparked and crackled with **static electricity**.

The first machine to make static electricity was invented in 1663 by Otto von Guericke (1602–1686). A large ball of yellow sulphur rubbed against a pad, making sparks. It was called a friction machine.

Word bank

capacitor device for storing electricity, also called a condenser
energy power or ability to be active and do something

Fizz, crackle, pop

In 1746, Dutch physics professor Pieter van Musschenbroek accidentally discovered how to store this mysterious electricity. He tried a **friction** machine with a wire running into a jar of water. His assistant wondered why the machine did not make sparks, touched the wire, and got a shock from electricity stored in the jar.

Musschenbroek did the same and wrote: "A shock of such violence shook my whole body, as by a lightning strike." He was the first to publish what he discovered about storing static electricity. The jar was named the Leyden jar after the town where he lived.

Can you believe it?

In 1745 German scientist Ewald von Kleist touched his electric generator with a nail stuck through the cork of a bottle. He got a shock when he touched the nail. He didn't understand why, but somehow the bottle stored electricity. Kleist discovered this just before Musschenbroek made his Leyden jar, but he didn't report it and so he missed getting the credit.

This scientist's Leyden jar is made of a bottle of water with a brass rod dipped into it.

Just so you know

The Leyden jar was the earliest type of **capacitor** (a device for storing electricity). It worked like a simple battery, but it was a glass jar with a layer of metal foil on the outside and another layer on the inside.

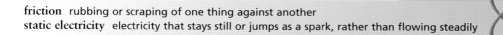

friction   rubbing or scraping of one thing against another
static electricity   electricity that stays still or jumps as a spark, rather than flowing steadily

Deadly shocks

Many scientists knew the electrical power of lightning was deadly, yet they still experimented with electricity in their **laboratories**. Some of them had to learn the hard way just how dangerous electricity can be. Physicists risked death when they made machines that produced and stored electrical **energy**.

Just so you know

Even a small electric **current** can kill, like touching a wire from the **mains**. Electric shocks cause jerking muscles, racing heart, severe burns or sudden death. The path that the electricity takes through a body gets very hot. Burns occur all along that path, including the skin where the current enters and leaves the body.

Nollet carried out many experiments to show that electricity passes through the body. Here he is second from the left, holding the Leyden jar in his right hand.

Word bank

current flow of something, like water or electricity

In an experiment in 1750, Franklin found that an iron needle carried away electricity stored in a metal ball.

Freaky Franklin

Benjamin Franklin (1706–1790) was the most famous American scientist of his day. He was fascinated by electricity, which he did not really understand. He called it "electrical fire" and suggested it might be some sort of invisible fluid. Many people thought he was foolish to try his wacky experiments.

Franklin wrote to a friend after one fright, describing how he had just done an experiment which he never wanted to repeat. He had two large glass jars, containing as much electrical fire as 40 small bottles, and accidentally touched a wire. Franklin described how the flash was "very great" and the crack "as loud as a pistol". It left a round swelling where the fire entered his body, the size of half a pistol bullet!

Shocking stuff

Today scientists know all about safety with electricity. They wear special gloves, face masks, and boots. Sometimes they wear all-over metal suits to protect themselves. The suit carries the electricity away from the body.

Lit up by lightning

Benjamin Franklin suspected that lightning was a massive leaping spark of electricity, but he wanted to prove it. In 1752 he and his 21-year-old son did a daringly dangerous experiment. They flew a kite in a thunderstorm. A metal wire on the kite attracted a small flash of lightning that shot down the wet string and sizzled into a Leyden jar, where it was stored. The experiment worked and proved that lightning was electrical power.

Franklin then invented the lightning rod or lightning **conductor** – a strip of copper metal put on tall buildings. It attracts lightning which shoots down it into the ground, preventing major damage to the building.

Benjamin Franklin and his son were lucky not to be killed in their dangerous experiment with lightning. Many other scientists were.

Word bank

conductor substance which carries something, like electricity or heat

Freaky, frazzled, and fried

Other scientists tried to copy Franklin's lightning experiment – but with different results. A year later, Russian scientist Georg Richmann tried to attract lightning with a wire on his house. The wire led to his **laboratory** where an iron bar hung over a bowl of water containing iron filings. He also had a dial to read the amount of electrical **current**.

As a storm approached, Richmann watched the dial. Suddenly a flash of blue and white fire shot from the bar and hit Richmann's head. A loud bang filled the room and he fell down dead. Experiment over.

Gone in a flash

Flying a kite in a storm is very dangerous. More than 150 years after Franklin's experiment, a Swedish scientist was killed by lightning while he flew a kite in a storm. Ole Engelstad's experiment in 1909 was one of many that ended in a flash of disaster.

Engelstad was due to sail with the famous explorer Roald Amundsen, but he was killed by deadly lightning. A mountain near the South Pole is named after him.

Shockers of their day

By the early 1800s scientists knew how to make **static electricity** from **friction** of some materials, and how to store electrical **energy** in a Leyden jar. They had also worked out that lightning was a sudden blast of electrical power, and that electricity could flow along a wire as a **current**, causing heat. Yet they still didn't know how to use an electric current as power.

In 1820 in Denmark, Hans Christian Oersted found that an electric current caused a nearby **magnetic** compass needle to move. This meant the electric current produced a magnetic **force**. Until then no one knew that magnetism and electricity are closely related. This was a tremendous breakthrough.

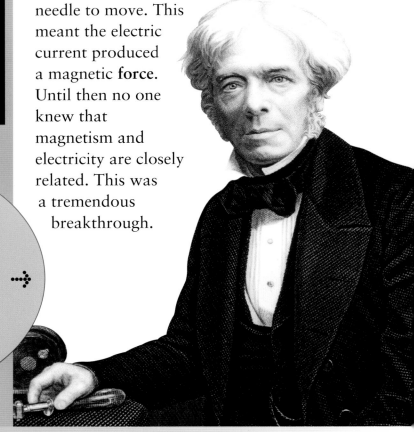

Hair-raising times

Static electricity can make people's hair stand on end. A generator makes static which is stored in a metal dome. When anyone touches the dome, the electricity travels to their hair. As each hair receives the static, it pushes away or repels the others, causing all the hairs to stand on end.

Michael Faraday made many advances in our understanding of electricity. He is known as one of the greatest experimenters in the history of science.

Word bank

cell in physics, device for making electricity from chemicals
dynamo machine that makes or generates electricity

Making power

Michael Faraday (1791–1867) was a British scientist whose experiments with electricity led to great things. Knowing that an electric current could cause a magnetic field, he believed a magnetic field could produce an electric current. He proved this in 1831 – a landmark in science. It led to the **dynamo**, which produces a constant flow of electricity.

In 1836 Faraday showed how people could be shielded from electricity if they sat in a metal cage. Instead of entering the cage, electricity flowed through the outside bars. Inside the cage it was scary but perfectly safe.

This modern Faraday cage works in the same way as Faraday's original design. The bars carry away the electricity, so the person inside is safe.

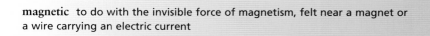

magnetic to do with the invisible force of magnetism, felt near a magnet or a wire carrying an electric current

33

Curiosity killed the cat (almost)

Thomas Alva Edison (1847–1931) was one of the United States' most important inventors, even though he tried some weird and wacky ideas. As a boy he was curious about everything. At the age of ten years, he set up a **laboratory** in his bedroom. Even then he was interested in **static electricity**. So he attached wires to the tails of two cats and quickly rubbed their fur. Nothing happened – much to the relief of the cats, as the experiment could have been dangerous and cruel.

Floating friend

Edison did some strange things. As a boy, he made a friend swallow **laxative** powders which fizzed when mixed with water. He hoped the bubbles would make gas in his friend's stomach and cause him to float in the air. It didn't work! Later, when Edison got married, he was so busy inventing that he almost forgot his own wedding.

In 1871 Thomas Edison's bride Mary came to drag him away from his scientific work, so they could get married.

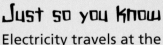

Just so you know

Electricity travels at the speed of light – almost 300,000 kilometres per second (186,000 miles per second). This means it could go around the world seven times in less than one second.

Word bank

eccentric acting or thinking in an unusual way
laxative medicine to make you need the toilet soon after taking it

Electric light

Edison's curiosity lasted all his life and led to many inventions. In 1877 he invented a light bulb that stayed lit for far longer than previous bulbs. He had spent two years experimenting with different materials which glow when electricity passes through them. They included his own hair, coconut hair, horsehair, straw, and fishing line. At last he used a specially treated piece of cotton thread and the light bulb worked.

In 1881 Edison built a large **dynamo** that could power 1,200 light bulbs at once. It was installed in the first central power station in London, England. The following year he opened the United States' first big electricity generator at the Pearl Street Station in Manhattan, New York.

Another electrical bright spark

In his United States laboratory Nikola Tesla (1856–1943) was also experimenting with electricity. He lit up lamps by letting electricity flow right through his body! The Tesla coil, which he invented in 1891, is used in radios, televisions, and other electronic equipment. Tesla was so **eccentric** that he always walked around a building three times before going inside.

This huge modern Tesla coil makes mini-lightning – 60 sparks per second with a power of more than one million volts.

Making waves

Newton's nightmare

In 1692 Isaac Newton was writing a book about light and colour. While he was out of his study, his dog knocked a candle on to his papers. Many years' work on light went up in flames. Newton was so upset that he gave up science for two years. It took him another ten years to re-write his book, which marked an important advance in the science of light.

Physics can sometimes seem foolish because it studies things we can't see. Scientists long ago could only see the effects of **forces** such as gravity, electricity, and **magnetism**, but they could never look at such things under a microscope. They also tried to understand how light, sound, and other "waves" travelled through the air. Although they couldn't see how these waves moved, they discovered some amazing science.

Just so you know

A wave is the movement of electrical and magnetic forces, or of tiny particles in a substance such as air or water. As the wave travels, it carries **energy** from place to place.

Newton had a breakdown after his scientific notes for a book were accidentally burned. He finally finished the book, called *Opticks*, in 1704.

Word bank

prism   piece of clear glass or plastic with flat angled sides

Let there be light

For centuries scientists tried to understand how light travels and why it has different colours. Apart from his work on gravity and motion, Isaac Newton also studied light. He shone sunlight through a **prism** (triangular piece of glass) and found that it is made up of many colours. He asked such questions as: "How can you see a light from many miles away in the dark?" He believed light moved through the air as a stream of tiny particles.

About a hundred years later, another British scientist dared to argue with Netwon's ideas. Thomas Young (1773–1829) shone a bright light through two small slits on to a screen and saw a pattern of stripes. This made him think that light travels through the air as waves. He was spot on!

When Newton shone a light through a prism, he saw it split into the colours of the rainbow. A similar effect happens with light shining on to a modern CD or DVD.

Waves from far away

The world of sound has always fascinated scientists. It was only by finding out how sound works and travels through the air, that scientists could develop telephones, recording equipment, and radios.

As early as AD 1500, Leonardo da Vinci described sound moving in waves. In 1600 Galileo studied how strings **vibrate** to make sounds. By 1687 Isaac Newton published a scientific report on sound.

German physicist Heinrich Hertz worked on radio waves. In 1887 he sent them over several metres. Italian scientist Guglielmo Marconi wondered if radio waves could be sent much further through the air. By 1899 he had developed a radio **transmitter** to send the first radio or "wireless" signals from England to France. Soon sounds could be turned into radio signals and sent long distances to radio **receivers**, which changed the signals back into sounds.

Recording sound

Can you imagine life without music at the press of a button? Thomas Edison experimented with a machine to record sounds in 1877. He called it the phonograph. Before long the world of scratchy sound records had begun.

In Edison's phonograph, sound waves vibrated a needle that scratched a wavy groove into a cylinder. When the needle passed along the groove again, it vibrated the attached funnel and played back the sounds.

Word bank

eardrum thin layer inside the ear that vibrates when sounds hit it
receiver device that receives things, usually radio signals

Can you believe it?

Today we have the technology to receive radio signals in our mouths! A tiny phone that picks up radio signals can fit inside a tooth. Then vibrations travel along the jawbone to a person's ear for an instant message. Some people have even picked up sound signals in their tooth fillings!

Just so you know

Sound waves travel through air at about 330 metres per second (1,083 feet per second) – one million times slower than light. The waves make our **eardrums** vibrate and our brains translate those vibrations into the sounds we hear.

Did you know?

Sound waves can even break glass. Some opera singers with very high-pitched voices have been able to shatter wine glasses by singing a single note into a microphone next to them. Warning – loud music not only breaks glass, it also damages eardrums.

Very loud sounds can make substances like glass vibrate so much, they shake themselves to pieces.

transmitter   device that sends out radio signals
vibrate   move or shake to and fro, usually quite fast

Exciting X-rays

An accident brought about an amazing discovery in 1895. One night, German physicist Wilhelm Röntgen (1845–1923) saw a screen glow in his **laboratory** as he made sparks in a tube. As he moved he stopped in surprise. He saw shadows of his bones on the screen. Mysterious rays had passed through his hand. As he didn't know what these weird rays were, he just called them X-rays – the "X" meaning "unknown".

Just so you know

X-rays are waves of electrical and **magnetic energy** that cannot be seen. Light is similar energy but the waves can be seen, and they are longer than X-rays. Radio waves are also electro-magnetic and have even longer waves.

William Röntgen studies a young patient using an early X-ray machine. In 1901 he was awarded the Nobel Prize in Physics for his discovery.

Word bank

photographic film thin layer or sheet that detects patterns of light by chemical changes

Saving lives

Unable to believe what he saw, Wilhelm used **photographic film** to make a record. He called his wife and asked her to hold up her hand. The image showed the bones in her hand and her wedding ring, but no flesh. X-rays were a great discovery because they could show what was happening inside someone's body. Within a year doctors were making the first images of broken bones, even though still no one knew what the mysterious rays were.

Today doctors can even examine blood vessels inside patients by injecting them with a chemical that shows up on an X-ray. Moving X-ray images can also be recorded on video. Wilhelm Röntgen's amazing accident has saved many thousands of lives.

Dangerous waves

Polish physicist Marie Curie (1867–1934) knew that X-rays could kill some cancer **cells**. However, they also harmed ordinary body cells. Marie won prizes for her important discoveries but later she died of cancer – caused by her repeated work with dangerous rays. Today X-rays in hospitals are carefully controlled to stop them causing harm.

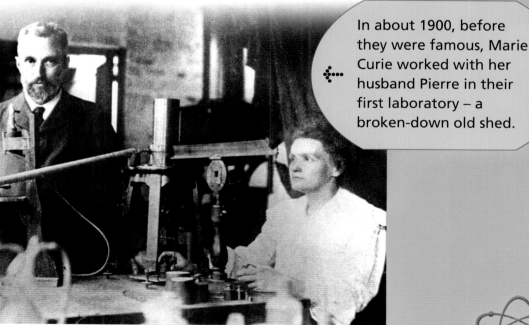

In about 1900, before they were famous, Marie Curie worked with her husband Pierre in their first laboratory – a broken-down old shed.

cell in biology, microscopic part or "building block" of a living thing

Magic microwaves

In World War II, scientists developed a way of detecting where enemy planes were flying at night. This used types of radio waves and was called **radar**. It needed a device called a **magnetron** that sent out high-**energy** radio signals with short waves, called microwaves. Then, in 1946, American scientist Percy Spencer was testing a magnetron tube when he got a strange feeling. He reached into his pocket and felt a warm gooey mess where a bar of chocolate had been. Microwaves had melted the chocolate.

Physics and ready-meals

Where would modern kitchens be without a microwave oven to heat or cook food in seconds? A device called a magnetron inside the oven directs microwaves on to the food. The waves make water and fat in the food **vibrate** so fast that they make heat, which quickly cooks the food.

Just so you know

Microwaves are electro-**magnetic** energy, like X-rays, light, and radio waves. Their waves are longer than the waves of light, but shorter and with more energy than radio waves.

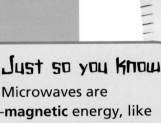

In 1947 one of the first ever microwave ovens was the Raytheon Radarange. Cooking a hamburger sandwich took just 15 seconds.

magnetron machine that uses magnetic and electric energy to make microwaves

Splat!

When Percy held a bag of corn next to the magnetron, each piece began to pop into a puffy shape – popcorn! He put an egg beside the magnetron and the shell began to crack. He called another scientist to come and look closely. Suddenly the egg exploded and splattered hot yolk all over their stunned faces!

If an egg cooked that quickly by microwave energy, why couldn't other foods? Spencer set to work making a microwave oven. It was huge, standing almost 2 metres (6.5 feet) tall, but it worked. However it took many more years before microwave ovens became small enough for ordinary kitchens.

Mobile phones rely on low-power microwaves. They were only developed after lots of physics research, over hundreds of years.

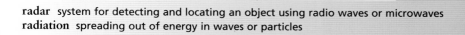

radar system for detecting and locating an object using radio waves or microwaves
radiation spreading out of energy in waves or particles

43

Yesterday, today, and tomorrow

Freaky and sometimes foolish physics is still alive and well. Big ideas and weird science have been part of recent discoveries as well as projects for the future.

Over the last hundred years, the name of Albert Einstein has been known around the world. His mind-boggling ideas about physics changed the way scientists thought about light, **energy, mass,** and time. Many scientists called him a **genius.** In 1905 Einstein published his "**theory** of **relativity**". It showed how a moving object changes its size and mass depending on its speed. Even time can go faster or slower. Wow – that takes some thinking about!

Did you know?

Albert Einstein (1879–1955) was a German-Swiss-American physicist whose ability in mathematics was outstanding – even though he failed his maths school exam. Because he could not read well when young, some teachers thought he was below average and would never have a proper career. They were very wrong.

More than 50 years after his death, Einstein is one of the few scientists that most people know something about.

Word bank

mass amount of matter or substance in an object
nuclear physics branch of physics that studies the structure of atoms

The nuclear age

Between 1905 and 1925, Einstein changed scientists' understanding of nature, from the smallest **atom** to the whole Universe. His work led to some amazing science called **nuclear physics**. As scientists discovered more about nuclear physics, they realized that by "splitting atoms" they could release huge amounts of energy.

Einstein was not so sure that nuclear energy was possible. In 1932 he said: "There is not the slightest indication that nuclear energy will ever be obtainable. It would mean that the atom would have to be shattered at will."

For once, Einstein was wrong. Much electricity today is made from nuclear energy.

Can you believe it?

Although Einstein was very clever, he could be **eccentric**. Once he got lost and had to phone his secretary to ask the way home! He also told scientists they could study his brain after his death. So when he died, aged 76, his brain was sliced into 240 pieces and examined. Interestingly, his brain was about one-sixth wider than average.

The idea for making electricity in nuclear power stations came from work by Albert Einstein and other physicists.

relativity depending on or related to something else

Mind-boggling problems

Finding the answer to the world's energy needs has been a problem for many years. There are risks of **pollution**, of **fossil fuels** running out, and of a terrible nuclear accident. Physics today faces questions such as: How will the world get energy for the rest of the 21st century? Could we ever run cars on air or make electricity from sea water?

In the 1980s scientists in Utah, United States had been working on a way to make cheap, easy energy. In 1989 they said they had an answer. They claimed to have solved the world's energy problems by a new kind of physics called "cold **fusion**".

Physics has produced countless useful machines and gadgets, but also the terrible weapon of the atomic bomb.

Word bank

fossil fuels fuels such as coal, oil, and natural gas that formed inside Earth over a long time from plant or animal remains

Stanley Pons and Martin Fleischmann said they had discovered an amazing new source of energy by "cold fusion". They were mistaken.

Faulty physics

Everyone was amazed that energy could be made by joining **atoms** when cold, rather than splitting them when hot in nuclear power. This was a great breakthrough. Then the problems began. The scientists who did the experiment had made a mistake. Later they and other scientists were unable to repeat the first results. So physics is still not without its faults.

Some scientists still disagree about energy, pollution, and global warming. Most experts say that burning fuel is heating up the planet, causing ice caps to melt and the oceans to rise. However others warn that smoke pollution is cutting out sunlight. This might gradually make Earth cooler, starting another ice age. Whoever is right, today's physics still has big problems to solve.

Accidents

Even the most advanced physics can go wrong when people make mistakes. There have been dangerous accidents, despite all the safety measures in nuclear power stations. In 1986 an explosion at the Chernobyl nuclear power station in Ukraine affected much of Northern Europe. People today are still suffering from the harmful **radiation** this caused.

fusion joining together parts of atoms to release great amounts of energy
pollution chemicals, particles or rubbish that spoil or damage nature

Science fact or science fiction?

What was once thought to be silly science fiction sometimes becomes science fact. News that people could pay to go on holiday in space seemed like another make-believe story. However, it was true.

Space tourist arrives at ISS

In 2005 American space tourist Gregory Olsen took a 10-day trip to the ISS, International Space Station in a Russian rocket. Olsen is the third person to holiday on the ISS. It's thought he paid up to £11 million. He took part in studies of space sickness and helped the crew with medical experiments.

Lasers

Physics has developed amazing modern **lasers**, which were once the stuff of science fiction. A laser beam uses a special form of light. (LASER stands for Light Amplification by the Stimulated Emission of Radiation.) Lasers are used in CD and DVD players, dentists' drills, medical surgery, high-speed metal cutting machines, measuring devices and many other machines.

Space tourist Gregory Olsen (left) said after his trip: "I had no idea that I would be flooded with such amazement and joy after seeing my first sunrise and sunset from space."

asteroid one of thousands of small planet-like objects in space, from a few metres to many kilometres across

Foolish future for physics?

Believe it or not, you might be able to wear an invisible cloak soon! Japanese scientists have created a cloak that makes it possible to "see" straight through its wearer. Slip it on and you become "invisible". The fabric is made up of **reflective** material coated with tiny beads. It is fitted with cameras that project what is at the back of the wearer on to the front. The effect is to make the wearer blend into the background and disappear. The cloaks could be in the shops soon (if only you could see them!).

Whatever will the weird world of freaky and sometimes foolish physics come up with next?

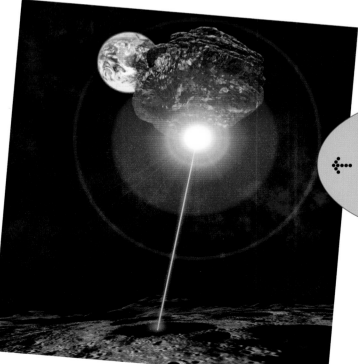

Will physics save Earth?

Some scientists think an **asteroid** will hit Earth in 2036. The 390-metre (1,300-foot) wide Apophis Asteroid may hit our planet with a huge blast, causing great damage. Could laser beams be used against it? A laser "strike" on the icy-cold asteroid might release gas which would fire it off course, away from Earth. Phew!

Will laser beams based on the Moon zap the next large asteroid that heads for Earth?

laser device that produces a special kind of pure, powerful light
reflective returning of light or sound waves which bounce off a surface

Physics timeline

400 BC	Democritus develops the **theory** that **matter** is made of tiny particles he calls *atomos*
250 BC	Archimedes develops the principles of buoyancy and levers
1086	First description of a **magnetic** compass by Chinese scientist Shen Kua
1480	**Reflection** of light is studied by Leonardo da Vinci, who also designs flying machines
1604	A major work on optics (the science of light) is published by Johannes Kepler
1609	Galileo Galilei constructs his own telescope and starts his series of discoveries, including the four largest moons of Jupiter, craters on the Moon and "handles" on the planet Saturn, which turned out to be its rings
1660	A **static electricity** generator is invented by Otto von Guericke
1665	Isaac Newton began his work on laws of gravity and motion, and his study of light and its colours
1745–46	Leyden jars are invented independently by Ewald von Kleist and Pieter van Musschenbroek
1752	Benjamin Franklin performs his famous "kite experiment", showing that lightning is electricity
1783	One of the Montgolfier brothers' hot-air balloons rises to an altitude of more than 1.5 kilometres (1 mile)
1800	The voltaic **cell** or "Volta's pile" is invented by Alessandro Volta; it is an early type of battery
1831	The **dynamo** is invented by Michael Faraday
1853	George Cayley builds a person-carrying glider

1865	James Clerk Maxwell proves that electro-magnetic waves travel at the speed of light
1877	Thomas Edison invents the light bulb
1887	Heinrich Hertz predicts the existence of radio waves and successfully detects them a year later
1888	Nikola Tesla designs alternating **current** (AC) power generators
1897	A radio message is sent by Guglielmo Marconi more than 30 kilometres (19 miles) from the Isle of Wight to Dorset, England
1901	Thomas Edison invents the storage battery
1903	The Wright brothers achieve the first powered person-carrying flight
1905	Albert Einstein puts forward his **theory** of special **relativity**
1910	The first movie pictures with sound are developed by Thomas Edison
1926	The first liquid-fuel rocket is launched by Robert Goddard
1969	The first **astronauts** walk on the Moon
1981	IBM release their first PC, or Personal Computer
2001	Astronomers discover a star cluster 13.4 billion light years from Earth, the farthest object ever located and "at the edge of the detectable universe"
2003	Apple launch the iPod personal music player
2006	Scientists build a pinhead-sized artificial eye containing 8,500 lenses, which could be used in ultra-thin cameras or to develop light-detecting microchips for the eyes of blind people

Find out more

Using the Internet

Explore the Internet to find out more about the history of physics or to see pictures of famous physicists and their work.

You can use a search engine such as **www.yahooligans.com**

Or ask a question at **www.ask.com**

Type in key words such as
- Galileo Galilei
- gravity
- history of flight
- firsts in space travel
- electricity
- Albert Einstein

Websites that explore the life and work of Benjamin Franklin include **www.ushistory.org/franklin**

Find the latest space news and topics from NASA at **www.nasa.gov/audience/forkids/home/index.html**

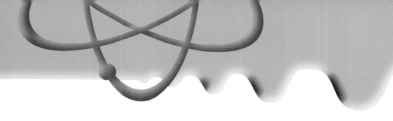

Books

You can find out more about strange science and foolish physics by looking at other books.

Ade, Chris; Wertheim, Jane; and Stockley, Corinne. *The Usborne Illustrated Dictionary of Physics* (Usborne, 2002)

Arnold, Nick. *Horrible Science: Explosive Experiments* (Scholastic Books, 2001)

Arnold, Nick. *Horrible Science: Suffering Scientists* (Scholastic Books, 2000)

Chapman, Steven. *Energy Essentials: Energy Transfers* (Raintree, 2005)

Parker, Steve. *Tabletop Scientist: Electricity and Magnetism* (Raintree, 2005)

Internet search tips

There are billions of pages on the Internet so it can be difficult to find exactly what you are looking for.

These search tips will help you find websites more quickly:

- Know exactly what you want to find out about first.
- Use two to six keywords in a search, putting the most important words first.
- Be precise. Only use names of people, places, or things.

Nasty noise for teens

A new gadget that makes a high-pitched noise is stopping teenage gangs from hanging around street corners in parts of the UK. It sends out 80-decibel bursts of very high-frequency pulsing sounds. Called the STD, Sonic Teenage Deterrent, it can only be heard by the under-20s because their hearing is more sensitive – older people cannot hear it at all. The STD annoys teenagers so much that they have to clutch their ears and move away.

Glossary

asteroid one of thousands of small planet-like objects in space, from a few metres to many kilometres across

astrology non-scientific study of how stars are meant to affect human lives and relationships

astronaut traveller in space

astronomer scientist who studies stars, moons, planets, and other space objects

astrophysics branch of science dealing with physical and chemical measurements of stars and other huge objects in space

atom smallest piece or particle of a substance

calculation detailed mathematical work

capacitor device for storing electricity, also called a condenser

cell in physics, a device for making electricity from chemicals. In biology, a microscopic part or "building block" of a living thing.

conductor substance which carries something, like electricity or heat

current flow of something, like water or electricity

density amount of material or matter in a certain volume

dynamo machine that makes or generates electricity

eardrum thin layer inside the ear that vibrates when sounds hit it

eccentric acting or thinking in an unusual way

energy power or ability to be active and do something

force push or pull that makes things move or change direction

formula process or rule written as numbers, letters, and symbols

fossil fuels fuels such as coal, oil, or natural gas that formed inside Earth over a long time from plant or animal remains

friction rubbing or scraping of one thing against another

fusion joining together parts of atoms to release great amounts of energy

genius very gifted person with great abilities

indivisible impossible to split into smaller parts

laboratory scientific work place for experiments, called a "lab"

laser device that produces a special kind of pure, powerful light

laxative medicine to make you need the toilet soon after taking it

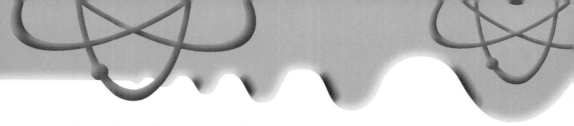

magnetic to do with the invisible force of magnetism, felt near a magnet or a wire carrying an electric current

magnetron machine that uses magnetic and electric energy to make microwaves

mains powerful electricity we use when we plug into wall sockets

mass amount of matter or substance in an object

matter substance made of atoms and similar particles

NASA National Aeronautics and Space Administration, responsible for the space programme of the United States since 1958

nuclear physics branch of physics that studies the structure of atoms

photographic film thin layer or sheet that detects patterns of light by chemical changes

pollution chemicals, particles or rubbish that spoil or damage nature

prism piece of clear glass or plastic with flat angled sides

probe small unmanned spacecraft

properties qualities or features, like being hard or soft

propulsion pushing power, a force that makes something move

radar system for detecting and locating an object using radio waves or microwaves

radiation spreading out of energy in waves or particles

receiver device that receives things, usually radio signals

reflective returning of light or sound waves which bounce off a surface

relativity depending on or related to something else

Solar System planets, moons and other objects that go around the Sun

static electricity electricity that stays still or jumps as a spark, rather than flowing steadily

theory general idea to explain how something happens

transmitter device that sends out radio signals

vibrate move or shake to and fro, usually quite fast

Index

Titles in the *Weird History of Science* series include:

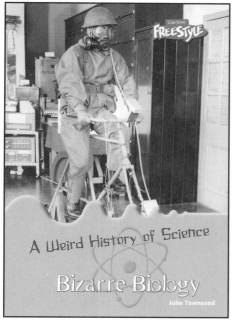

A Weird History of Science
Bizarre Biology
John Townsend

Hardback 978-1-4062-0556-5

A Weird History of Science
Crazy Chemistry
John Townsend

Hardback 978-1-4062-0558-9

A Weird History of Science
Foolish Physics
John Townsend

Hardback 978-1-4062-0557-2

A Weird History of Science
Outrageous Inventions
John Townsend

Hardback 978-1-4062-0559-6

Find out about the other titles in this series on our website www.raintreepublishers.co.uk